# Stagecoach Days and Stagecoach Kings

# Stagecoach Days
# and Stagecoach Kings

BY VIRGINIA VOIGHT

ILLUSTRATED BY CARY

**AEP**

AMERICAN EDUCATION PUBLICATIONS / A XEROX COMPANY

Middletown, Connecticut

## Picture credits:

*Stagecoach Days and Stagecoach Kings* is one of a group of books published by Garrard Publishing Co., Champaign, Illinois 61820. Other similar books are available in reinforced library bindings from Garrard Publishing Co.

American Education Publications Paperback Edition
Published by arrangement with Garrard Publishing Co.

1 2 3 4 5 / 75 74 73 72 71

# Contents

## 1. Early Days on the Road

Tree stumps and rocks made the early roads through the American wilderness dangerous. There were few taverns, except in towns. On long trips people often had to camp overnight in the woods. Bears, panthers, and wolves made any trip a perilous adventure. Sometimes a little group of people on horseback would join a postrider on his mail-delivery trips between colonies, paying him for his protection and help on the journey.

Such trips were dreaded by travelers, especially in stormy weather. Covered vehicles were needed and, also, well-spaced wayside inns where travelers could get food and shelter.

Stagecoaches were unknown in those days. Better roads had to be made before any kind of four-wheeled vehicle could be used outside of towns. The first step in this direction came when the governments of the different colonies began to encourage farmers to pay their taxes by working on the roads. The workmen widened the trails and filled in some of the boggy places with gravel. They also built bridges across some of the smaller rivers. Ferries were established to carry traffic across the wider streams. Each year the roads improved a little, but it wasn't until shortly before the War for Independence that anyone was brave enough to attempt to run stagecoaches.

The first public transportation vehicles in the colonies were clumsy and slow and built like farm wagons. They traveled for only short distances, and the service they gave was so irregular that few people used them. But they marked the beginning of a new and more convenient way to travel, and one that improved gradually over the years.

The word stagecoach originated from the fact that the coaches and wagons used for

This crude country inn was a relay stop for "stage wagons" in the early days of the republic.

public transportation, and the sleighs used in the northern colonies in winter, all stopped at regularly spaced stages along their routes to have their teams changed for fresh horses. These relay stops were made at wayside inns and village taverns that boarded stagecoach teams in their stables. The coming of stagecoaches, with horses to be cared for and passengers to be fed, meant new prosperity for many a sleepy village inn. And in time new inns were opened to serve the ever-growing stagecoach lines.

## To the PUBLIC.

THE FLYING MACHINE, kept by John Mercereau, at the New Blazing-Star-Ferry, near New-York, sets off from Powles Hook every Monday, Wednesday, and Friday Mornings, for Philadelphia, and performs the Journey in a Day and a Half, for the Summer Season, till the 1st of November; from that Time to go twice a Week till the first of May, when they again perform it three Times a Week. When the Stages go only twice a Week, they set off Mondays and Thursdays. The Waggons in Philadelphia set out from the Sign of the George, in Second-street, the same Morning. The Passengers are desired to cross the Ferry the Evening before, as the Stages must set off early the next Morning. The Price for each Passenger is *Twenty Shillings*, Prop. and Goods as usual. Passengers going Part of the Way to pay in Proportion.

As the Proprietor has made such Improvements upon the Machines, one of which is in Imitation of a Coach, he hopes to merit the Favour of the Publick.

JOHN MERCEREAU.

John Mercereau adopted the name of Flying Machine for his stagecoach, too. He announced in 1771 that he could "perform the journey" from New York to the city of Philadelphia in a day and a half.

John Butler was the most ambitious of the pioneer stagemen of America. In 1766 he boldly announced that he was establishing an "express" stagecoach service between New York and Philadelphia.

It took four days for a horseman to make the journey between these two cities, so people could hardly believe John Butler's boast that his stagecoach, which he named the "Flying Machine," would take only two days. However, a full load of nine passengers turned up at the New York tavern where tickets were sold for the first trip of the Philadelphia coach.

No one knows who those first Flying Machine passengers were. There may have been a young Yale or Harvard graduate on his way to take a post as teacher in a Philadelphia school. A hairdresser, carrying tongs and boxes of hair powder in his carpet-bags, might have been going to seek work with the ladies and gentlemen of Philadelphia, then the largest and richest city in America. And there might have been a couple who had always wanted to travel but who had had no way to get about until now. To them the hundred-mile stagecoach journey would have seemed as adventurous as a trip to the moon.

The stagecoach standing before the door of the tavern was only a springless wagon with a cloth top and no windows. The front and back were open, but there were curtains that could be rolled down in stormy weather. The words "Flying Machine—New York to Philadelphia" were painted in bold letters on the sides.

To enter this stagecoach one had to climb over the high front wheels with their thick iron tires. Men scrambled in somehow; a lady in full, flouncy skirts had more trouble. She set her foot on a spoke of the wheel and another passenger boosted her from behind while the driver grasped her outstretched hand and hauled her up to his seat. Then she had to crawl over the plank seats, straddling each one until she came to the one assigned to her.

Inside the stagecoach there was barely room for nine passengers to huddle together on the hard backless planks set crossways in the wagon. The passengers held some of their luggage on their laps and stowed the rest of it under their legs. This gave them so little room that, at the end of the day's ride, they were lame from kinks and cramps.

Although the roads had been somewhat improved, they were still very poor. Stretches of

"corduroy" had been laid over some of the swampy sections. Corduroy roads were made by laying logs crossways and close together. These wooden roads kept the Flying Machine from sinking into the mud, but they were far from smooth, and the passengers were always badly shaken up.

On wet stretches where no corduroy had been laid, the stagecoach often got stuck, and the male passengers had to get out and push. After they had the Flying Machine back on firm ground, they would climb back to their seats, weary and mud-spattered. But then the stagecoach might come to a hill, and the driver would shout for everyone to get out and walk to ease the load for the horses.

On roads where ruts were worn deep, great care had to be taken to balance the stagecoach and keep it from upsetting. If it began to tip to the right, the driver shouted for the passengers to lean to the left. Then as the wagon lurched into another rut, he would yell frantically, "Lean to the right!" The passengers would then quickly fling themselves so far to the right that some of them tumbled off their seats. A day of such rugged traveling was exhausting.

At some inns a fiddler's gay tune and a merry dance
made weary travelers forget poor food and beds.

The wayside inns were almost as dreary as
the roads. Food was distasteful at most inns.
Travelers wrote in letters and diaries that the
bedrooms were swarming with bugs. There
were no private rooms. Strangers had to sleep
two or three in a bed in rooms crowded with
ten or twelve beds. No one undressed, but
signs on the walls requested that guests "re-
move boots before retiring."

After the colonies had won their independence from England, many stage wagons of
the same type as the Flying Machine began

running between the larger towns of the new United States. Because of the bumping endured by the suffering passengers, people called these stagecoaches "spankers." But brighter days were ahead.

Levi Pease was the first "stagecoach king" in America. He started his stageline with two crude stage wagons that ran between Connecticut and Massachusetts, but before many years had passed, he had stagelines running north into New Hampshire and as far south as Georgia. Captain Pease introduced the first touch of glamour to stagecoaching. He had his drivers blow a melodious horn when the stagecoach was approaching an inn where the horses were to be changed.

Until the time of Levi Pease, the United States mail was delivered by postriders. Captain Pease persuaded the Post Office Department that the mail would be safer and faster if it were carried by stagecoach. He received the first mail contract ever given out by the government and made the first mail delivery by stagecoach in January 1786.

This was an important date for stagecoaching. To run a successful stageline, the owner had to spend huge sums of money on horses, equipment, drivers, and maintenance. Passenger fares did not bring in nearly enough money. The existence of long-distance stagecoach lines depended on the money received from the government for carrying the mail.

Roads in the eastern United States kept on improving, and this inspired carriage makers to build better stagecoaches. The new coaches looked less like wagons and were a little more comfortable than the Flying Machine. Doors were set in the sides, and little steps made it easier for passengers to climb aboard. A luggage carrier was bolted to the rear to carry the mail bags and the passengers' luggage.

This Trenton stagecoach was more attractive than the Flying Machine, but passengers still had a rough ride.

Wayside inns improved in quality, also, as they competed for the business of the many new stagelines. At the better inns, rooms were cleaner and more comfortable and, often, travelers could get private rooms. Innkeepers now took pride in serving tasty food to stagecoach travelers.

At noon or overnight stops, travelers trooped eagerly into the big dining room of a wayside inn. The log fire sent out a cheery glow from the huge fireplace. The long table down the center of the room was an inviting sight, with its platters of roast beef and boiled ham, and bowls heaped with vegetables. Waitresses passed plates of hot biscuits and johnnycake, and generous wedges of mince, pumpkin, and apple pie. Tea, coffee, cider, and foaming flip, a strong, hot drink, were served. Usually a meal such as this would cost a quarter.

In spite of all the improvements, stagecoaches were still cramped, and most of them were rickety and poorly made. A long ride by stagecoach was still something to be endured rather than enjoyed. But Lewis Downing, a boy who lived in Newburgh, New York, would one day make stagecoaches both safe and comfortable.

## 2. Lewis Downing and the Concord Stagecoach

Lewis Downing arrived in the town of Concord, New Hampshire in the spring of 1813. He had just turned twenty-one.

Lewis had grown up in Newburgh, New York, where his father, a blacksmith and wheelwright, built wagons and repaired wagons and stagecoaches. Lewis had always liked to poke about the shop and watch his father make handhewn wheel spokes and fit iron tires to wagon and stagecoach wheels. Everything about wagons and stagecoaches interested him.

When Lewis finished school, he entered his father's shop as an apprentice wheelwright. He learned his craft well, and after he had become a skilled wheelwright, he worked a few years for his father and saved some money. As he worked, he dreamed of the day when he would open a wagon shop of his own. Now that day had come! The thriving town of Concord, in the midst of magnificent forests which would supply all kinds of wood, was an ideal place for a wagon shop.

Lewis would never forget the stagecoach journey from Newburgh to Concord, for it was one of the most unpleasant experiences of his life. The clumsy stagecoach was narrow and cramped, and its broken springs were a torment to the passengers as they jolted along. As Lewis tried to stretch his painfully kinked legs, he wondered, crossly, why the men who made stagecoaches didn't give some thought to the comfort of their passengers. Some day, he vowed to himself, he would make a stagecoach that would be both beautiful and comfortable.

Soon after he arrived in Concord, Lewis opened a woodworking and wagon shop. He would need some income while he was working on his first wagon so, as a side line, he made wooden household wares. In the Concord lumber yards he found plenty of fine-grained walnut, maple, and wild cherry for his woodenware, and tough hickory and oak for his wagon.

When he wasn't working on his wagon, he was turning out wooden bowls, spoons, clothes pegs, spindles for spinning wheels, and grooved washboards. Housewives bought them eagerly.

The future fame and prosperity of Lewis Downing and the stagecoach factory that he founded depended greatly on two work rules that he made at the very beginning. He promised himself that only the most skilled craftsmen would work on a Downing vehicle, and that they would use only the finest materials.

Lewis finished building his first wagon in the fall of 1813. He sold it promptly for sixty dollars, a high price for those days. He now felt confident enough to hire three men to help him in the wagon shop.

The wagon shed was a place of humming activity. It seemed as though every farmer and merchant who saw that first Downing wagon wanted one like it. Then a man placed an order for a buggy, and Lewis and his helpers made a fine job of the one-seated roofed carriage. The demand for Downing wagons and buggies became so great that Lewis had to enlarge his wagon shed.

Lewis had never forgotten his suffering as a stagecoach passenger. While his business was growing, Lewis kept working on plans for a perfect stagecoach. In 1826 he hired Stephen Abbot, a brilliant young craftsman, who had some sound ideas of his own about stagecoaches. The two men combined their ideas and together designed the wonderful Concord stagecoach which would soon become famous all over the world. To reward Stephen for his part in the work, Lewis made him a partner in the business. After that, the firm was known as Downing and Abbot.

An air of excitement hung over the wagon factory as the first Concord stagecoach took shape. Every part of this stagecoach, and of the thousands of other stagecoaches that would be built by Downing and Abbot in the years to come, was made by hand. Joiners, carpenters, wheelwrights, blacksmiths, painters, and upholsterers worked under the stern supervision of Lewis Downing. Lewis never allowed anything to interfere with his daily tour of the factory, and the craftsmen worked just a little harder when they saw the boss approaching. Lewis always carried a hammer on his inspection tours. If he saw a piece of shoddy work, his eyes would flash, and he would smash the offending work with a blow of his hammer.

STRAP
STRAP SEAT
FOOT
THOROUGHBRACES

"You have failed in your duty as a crafts-man!" he would thunder at the startled worker.

The wood used in Concord stagecoaches was carefully inspected to make sure that it was flawless; then it was cured for at least a year. This slow curing prevented any warping of the finished coaches. Concord stagecoaches always held their shape, even in the dry, punishing climate of the West, where other stagecoaches and wagons warped, shrank, and fell to pieces.

Instead of having metal springs which could

sag and break, Concord coaches were suspended on two thick straps made of many strips of strong, well-tanned leather. These straps were called "thoroughbraces." Concords swayed on them with such an easy motion that they were known as "rockaway" coaches on the highways of the eastern states.

Concord stagecoaches had doors and windows on both sides. Inside, well-cushioned leather seats provided room for nine passengers. Three passengers faced forward and three faced backward, on the permanent seats. Between them was the "strap seat." This center seat was kept hooked out of the way until the passengers took their places on the other seats; then it was lowered across the middle of the coach. A wide leather strap was stretched above it, shoulder high, to form a backrest. Several more passengers could ride outside on a seat just behind the driver's box.

Deep luggage carriers, called "boots," were placed at the front and rear of the stagecoaches. Mail bags, packages, and trunks were carried in the boots. Luggage that didn't fit into the boots was strapped to the flat top of the coach, where a metal railing prevented it from sliding off.

The stageline owners who bought Concord stagecoaches usually wanted portraits of famous men, or paintings of landscapes or animals on the stagecoach doors. John Borgum, a talented young artist, added these final touches to each stagecoach and framed the picture in curlicues and scrolls of gold leaf, scarlet, and green.

Brass fittings and decorative painting made Concord coaches as handsome as they were comfortable.

By now, many new and improved turnpikes made it possible to travel comfortably throughout most of the eastern states. There were dozens of new stagelines in operation, from the Atlantic coast to the Ohio River, and from Maine to Georgia. New stagecoaches were in demand. The Concord stagecoach was so handsome and gave such splendid service that other wagon factories began to copy its design. In time almost all stagecoaches were called "Concords." But no other stagecoach in the world ever equaled the Downing and Abbot coach for beauty, comfort, and the ability to withstand strain and hard wear.

There was one peril, however, from which even a Concord stagecoach could not protect its passengers, and that was the peril of stage-robbers.

In stagecoach days in New England and New York, horse thieves were more of a threat than stage robbers, because people in that part of the country usually carried bank drafts rather than large amounts of gold and silver. Horse thieves raided the stables of inns and relay stations to steal the fine stage horses. If they were caught, they were branded on the forehead with the letters HT. For a second offense, a horse thief was speedily hanged from a tree at some well-traveled crossroads.

But in Maryland and Pennsylvania, on the Great National Road that led over the mountains to the Ohio River, thousands of dollars were stolen from stagecoach passengers. A favorite place for a holdup was the top of a steep hill, where the horses would be pulling slowly. Suddenly two armed, masked men would step into the road. One would grab the reins of the nearer lead horse, the other would point his pistols at the stagecoach and order the driver to pull up. If the driver resisted, he was shot.

The robber then demanded that everyone get out of the stagecoach. He would hold out his hat and command all the gentlemen to toss their watches and money into it. Sometimes gallant robbers would permit the lady passengers to keep their jewelry. They would pull the mailbags out of the boot, bow politely to the ladies, and with pistols still leveled, back away into the shadow of the trees, where their horses were tied up. Then they would vault into their saddles and gallop away with their loot to some mountain hideaway where the law could seldom catch up with them.

## 3.  John Butterfield, King of the Road

While stagelines were expanding throughout the eastern United States, and stagecoaches were being improved until they reached the peak of perfection in the Concord coach, a boy was growing up in rural New York who would become the greatest stagecoach king of all.

In 1801, when John Butterfield was born, the United States was at the beginning of an exciting period of western expansion. All kinds of traffic flowed past the Butterfield farm on the Albany turnpike. Great canvas-covered freight wagons pulled by eight heavy horses were piled high with cloth, iron, guns, axes, and other goods on their way to settlers in

Indiana, Michigan, and Illinois, then the far western states of the union. Smaller covered wagons loaded with household gear and with bright-eyed children were driven by pioneers on their way to take up land in the West.

All this bustle of people moving to new homes and of freighters following the pioneers to supply them with things that they needed was made possible by the new roads that threaded the East. Stagecoaches, too, were an important part of the picture, as more and more people took advantage of public transportation. Young doctors and lawyers traveled to open offices in new towns and villages. Country people sending their children to school at town academies put the youngsters in the care of stagecoach drivers. Often, young couples would go on a honeymoon stagecoach trip.

Young Johnny Butterfield liked to sit on the farmyard fence and watch the colorful procession on the turnpike. Surely, he thought, there could be no finer sight than a stagecoach tearing along behind a racing four-horse team —especially the express coaches that carried the United States Mail!

The stagedriver sat on his box like a king on his throne. His twelve-foot whip was held aslant in his right hand, while with his left hand he controlled four sets of "ribbons" or reins. Beside him sat the conductor ready to sound a note of warning on the glittering stagehorn if any vehicle did not pull aside to let the mail express dash through. Johnny's face glowed with admiration as the stagecoach whirled past.

"Hallo-hallooo!" he shouted, waving his arm.

The era of stagecoaching in eastern United States was approaching its peak. The fine new turnpikes were surfaced with stone, making it possible for a stagecoach to flash along at a speed of ten miles an hour. Stagecoaches brought prosperity to towns and villages as new inns opened to accommodate the increased numbers of travelers. Men found employment at blacksmith shops that serviced stagecoaches and in the stables of inns. Women and girls were employed as cooks, waitresses, and chambermaids. Other women wove sheets and made quilts for the inns.

The stagecoach fare for a two-day trip from Albany to Boston or New York City was about six dollars. Fares were cheaper for those passengers who would get out and walk up hills where the horses found the going heavy.

# BOSTON,
## *Plymouth & Sandwich*
# MAIL STAGE,

### *CONTINUES TO RUN AS FOLLOWS:*

**LEAVES** Boston every Tuesday, Thursday, and Saturday mornings at 5 o'clock, breakfast at Leonard's, Scituate; dine at Bradford's, Plymouth; and arrive in Sandwich the same evening. Leaves Sandwich every Monday, Wednesday and Friday mornings; breakfast at Bradford's, Plymouth; dine at Leonard's, Scituate, and arrive in Boston the same evening.

Passing through Dorchester, Quincy, Wyemouth, Hingham, Scituate, Hanover, Pembroke, Duxbury, Kingston, Plymouth to Sandwich. *Fare* from Boston to Scituate, 1 doll. 25 cts. From Boston to Plymouth, 2 dolls. 50 cts. From Boston to Sandwich, 3 dolls. 63 cts.

N. B. Extra Carriages can be obtained of the proprietor's, at Boston and Plymouth, at short notice.—☞ STAGE BOOKS kept at Boyden's Market-square, Boston, and at Fessendon's, Plymouth.

**LEONARD & WOODWARD.**

BOSTON, *November 24, 1810.*

As food and service at wayside inns improved, stage-line operators advertised their stops to the public.

One of the drivers on the Albany run was famous as a "crack" reinsman, as stagedrivers were called. Captain Henry Buckley did not have a military title, but stagedrivers were so much admired and respected by the public that most of them were addressed as "captain."

In time, Captain Buckley began to watch for the friendly boy who waved to him from the farm fence. He even had his conductor blow a blast on the stagehorn to let Johnny know that they were coming. This was a great honor. Usually the stagehorn was sounded only to clear the road or when the coach was approaching a relay inn.

The thrilling notes of the stagehorn found an echo deep in young Johnny's heart. Long before he had grown up, he knew that he wanted to be a stagecoach driver like his hero, Captain Buckley.

John Butterfield was nineteen when he left the farm and went to Albany to find work with one of the stagelines that operated out of that city. Bronzed and rugged from working on the farm, he made a good impression when he strode into the office of the Parker Stagecoach Line and asked for a job.

"Can you handle horses?" the manager asked.

John nodded. "I've been driving horses since I was ten years old."

"We have a job open in our stables," the manager said.

This wasn't what John had in mind. "I want to be a stagedriver!"

The manager shook his head. "You haven't had enough experience for that. Our drivers are all crack reinsmen."

John gulped down his disappointment and started to turn away. "Wait!" the manager called out.

His shrewd eyes studied the clean-cut appearance and intelligent eyes of the young farmhand. "Take the stable job," he urged. "I'll send you out with some of our crack drivers on practice runs. When they say that you are ready, you can have a job as driver."

John thought a moment, then nodded. As a stable hand he would at least have a toehold in the stagecoach business!

In the Parker stables, he started at the humble task of cleaning out stalls, but soon became so useful that he was made boss of the stable crew.

John bought a blanket so that he could sleep in the hay in the stable loft. He ate only the plainest food. He was saving every possible penny, because now he had a new ambition. He was determined to have his own stageline!

True to his promise, the manager sent John out often as conductor on the company stage-coaches. It was the conductor's duty to collect fares, look after the passengers, and take charge of mail and express packages. But sometimes he took over the reins to give the driver a rest.

John learned how to hold four sets of reins laced between his fingers so he had each of the two leaders and each of the two wheelers of his team under perfect control at all times. He learned to handle the whip so that he could snap it out snaking and hissing to crack sharply above the head of a horse that wasn't pulling well. The whip was the symbol of a driver's authority over his team, but like most top stagedrivers, John never used it to lash his horses. Healthy, well-cared-for horses were only too eager to pull and to run. The worst they got from John Butterfield was a tickle with the tip of the lash to urge them to their best efforts.

At last the day came when John was told that he could have a job as stagedriver.

At a relay station passengers had only a few minutes
to stretch their legs as a new team was hitched up.

He was pleased because his run would be
along the highway he knew best, the great
Western Turnpike that led from Albany to the
Great Lakes. It was as if he sensed that his
greatest days in stagecoaching would be connected with the West.

Now it was John's turn to be "king of the
road," admired and cheered by boys as he
whirled along the highway or brought his team
sweeping up to a wayside inn. It was a proud
moment when he drove his stagecoach away

from the Albany station on his first morning as a full-fledged stagedriver.

"Give us a toot on your horn!" he urged the conductor, when they were half a mile from the first relay station.

The conductor lifted the stagehorn. "Ta-ta, ta-ta-ta." The music that John loved best echoed sweet and clear on the morning air.

John had kept his horses at a steady trot along the highway; now he snapped his whip to bring them into a gallop. They swept up to the inn in grand style. Two stablemen were waiting to unhitch the incoming team the moment that the stagecoach rolled to a stop. Two grooms rushed a fresh team from the inn stables.

"Good morning, Captain," called the innkeeper, bowing from the inn doorway.

John grinned happily at receiving this title. The fresh four-horse team was swiftly harnessed to the stagecoach. A groom tossed the reins up to John and jumped out of the way.

"Gid-ap!" John shouted, cracking his whip.

Away dashed the horses at an eager gallop.

John cut an elegant figure with his bell-crowned beaver hat worn at a jaunty angle and the silver buttons twinkling on his

greatcoat. Like most stagedrivers, he sported a scarlet silk sash around his waist. Fine clothes, befitting a crack reinsman, were his only extravagance. He saved most of his salary, and by the time he was twenty-one, he had enough money to buy a horse and buggy. Now, during his time off from his stagecoach job, he could make more money by running a livery, or taxi, service.

A few years later John was made manager of the Parker Stagecoach Line with a nice raise in pay. Several more years passed and the gold dollars piled up in his strongbox. At last he felt that he had saved enough to strike out for himself.

Organizing a stageline was a tremendous task. The first thing to do was to order stage-coaches. None would suit proud John Butterfield but those built by Downing and Abbot in Concord, New Hampshire. He found that a full outfit, including the stagecoach and harness and a team of four horses, cost one thousand dollars. He would need six stage-coaches and one hundred and fifty horses in order to start his stageline to western New York. The first run would be between Albany and Schenectady.

John ordered Morgan horses, bred in Vermont, for his stagecoach teams. This famous breed had the beauty and swiftness expected of the leaders of a team and, also, the staying power and strength needed from the hard-pulling wheelers. Most stagemen regarded Morgans as the finest stage horses in the world.

John made arrangements with the owners of wayside inns for the care and boarding of his relay teams and for meals and rooms for his passengers. The inns where Butterfield stagecoaches stopped would not be used by any other stageline. Each stageline advertised in waybills, tacked up in towns and villages to attract passengers, that its stagecoaches stopped only at the finest inns serving the tastiest food. Then if a stageline did not wish to lose its passengers to some other line, it had to make sure that the inns kept to a high standard of service.

John's hard work and careful planning made the Butterfield Stagecoach Line a success from the first, and as the years flew by, business increased until John owned most of the stagelines that ran west of Albany. Because of his splendid record in keeping to time schedules, he had no difficulty in getting mail contracts, and the money from these government contracts greatly increased his profits.

John felt keenly his responsibility in carrying the United States Mail. When one of his express mail coaches was about to pull away from the main station, he was usually on hand.

"Remember, boys!" he urged the driver and conductor, "nothing on God's earth must stop the United States Mail!" He said this so often that it became the company motto.

While John Butterfield was busy with his stagelines, a new era had opened in American transportation.

In 1830 the tiny locomotive "Tom Thumb" had started running on the new tracks of the Baltimore and Ohio Railroad and had run twelve miles in seventy-two minutes. At first the stagecoach kings of the eastern states shrugged off the railroad as something of a joke. But year after year, more track was laid and locomotives and railroad cars improved. Soon stagecoach passengers began to use the railroads. And to make matters worse, railroads were getting the mail contracts that meant so much to the stagelines! Stagelines were forced to shorten their runs, and many wayside inns had to close.

Early railroad cars looked like coaches on rails!

During these years of expanding railroads and fading stagelines in the eastern states, great events were taking place in the Far West.

In 1845 the United States admitted Texas into the Union as the twenty-eighth state. This meant war, for Mexico also claimed the territory of Texas. The two countries began a bitter struggle, which ended in 1848 with victory for the United States. The terms of the peace treaty provided that the United States should pay damages to Mexico, and the vast territory that included the future states of California, Arizona, New Mexico, Nevada, Utah, and Colorado was ceded to the United States. This far-flung new territory, which was now open to American settlers, had few roads except ancient Indian trails and buffalo traces. Stagecoaches and railroads were unknown there.

In the East, John Butterfield was still prosperous. He continued to run a number of branch stagelines that connected with the railroads, and he kept abreast of the times by investing money in the newly developed telegraph. But his heart was still in stagecoaching, and his thoughts kept turning to the new American territories in the Far West. He was sure that out there on the plains and in the mountains there were still years of service awaiting the stagecoach. And he longed to take part in the great adventure that was ahead.

## 4. Jim Birch and the Jackass Mail

At the time that John Butterfield was saving to start his stageline in New York, a boy was born in Massachusetts whose name would shine brightly on the roll of stagecoach kings.

Jim Birch was still in his teens when he got a job driving a stagecoach on the run between Boston and Providence, Rhode Island, where stagecoaches connected with New York steamboats. Speed was important. One passenger wrote:

"We were rattled from Providence to Boston in four hours, five minutes. If anyone wants to go faster, he may charter a streak of lightning."

Like many another crack reinsman, Jim Birch lost his job when the railroads began to take business away from the stagelines. He was twenty-one years old in 1849, when the newspapers were full of exciting accounts of the discovery of gold in California. Jim felt that a stageline might make a fortune in California. He bought a horse and joined a train of ox-drawn covered wagons for the trip across the plains to Sacramento, California. In his saddlebags he carried a tiny hoard of savings which he intended to invest in stage-coaching.

Sacramento was a bustling frontier town crowded with people on their way to the gold diggings. In the dusty streets Jim mingled with a crowd of gamblers in high hats, Chinese in pigtails and silken clothes, Mexicans in sombreros and bright serapes, and bearded miners in red flannel shirts and high boots. He learned that people were so anxious to get to the diggings and, once there, were so eager to receive mail from home and to send their gold dust out, that they would pay fantastic prices for transportation. He heard about a stagedriver who charged four dollars to deliver a letter and who made enormous profits

Shiploads of would-be miners put in at the bustling Sacramento waterfront, gateway to the gold fields.

hauling butter kegs filled with gold from the mines. As Jim had shrewdly guessed, transportation was the real, lasting bonanza of California.

Jim bought an old rancho wagon with board seats, and four half-wild mustangs, for which he paid four dollars apiece. Smiling broadly, he climbed into his wagon and drove to the boat landing on the Sacramento River. A ship from San Francisco had just docked. As the passengers came ashore, Jim shouted, "This way, gentlemen! All aboard for the gold diggings!"

In a few minutes his wagon was crowded with passengers.

Jim charged a passenger a dollar a mile, and he couldn't find room in his wagon to accommodate the people who fought for seats. His passengers were mostly miners, who sang, shouted, and whistled, while the wagon bumped wildly along behind Jim's fiery mustangs.

It was a small beginning, but soon Jim was able to buy more wagons, hire drivers, and lengthen his runs. Profits poured in. Within a year Jim was rich enough to order from Downing and Abbot some real stagecoaches, sent by clipper ship around Cape Horn. It was a proud day for Jim Birch when the clipper anchored in the river, and his splendid stagecoaches were paraded through Sacramento. He also bought some fine horses from traders who had driven them across country from Missouri.

In 1850, when California came into the Union, many stagelines began to operate in the rich new state. One of them was founded by Frank Stevens, an old friend of Jim's. Sacramento became a busy staging center and the competition was terrific among stagelines running to all points in California and also to Nevada and Mexico. There were price wars, and there were road races between rival companies. Sometimes a racing stagecoach would be forced off a narrow mountain road to crash with its passengers and horses in a rocky canyon far below.

In order to meet this fierce competition, Jim Birch and Frank Stevens combined their stagelines. Several other smaller companies joined them, and the Great California Stageline, largest stageline in the world, was formed. Jim became its first president. Four years later he suddenly retired from the stageline which had made him a millionaire at twenty-nine. He had an exciting new project in mind.

He had decided to put in a bid to the Post Office Department in Washington to carry the United States Mail across the country by stagecoach!

The people of California were clamoring for a fast reliable overland mail and passenger service. For some time there had been talk about the building of a transcontinental railroad to span the wilderness between Missouri and California, but so far this was only a subject for debate in Congress. Now Jim Birch set about forging the important link that would bind California to the other states.

The town of San Antonio, Texas was a stop for steamboats coming from the East Coast. The government at last authorized a route that could pick up mail from boats at San Antonio and run a stagecoach for mail and passengers from there to San Diego, California. There were to be mail deliveries twice each month.

The line would follow an old wagon trail that had been blazed by the United States Army during the Mexican War. It passed through wilderness country that was claimed by the Comanche Indians in Texas and the Apache in Arizona.

In 1857 the Post Office Department gave Jim Birch the mail contract for this route.

The scouts, army men, and pioneers with whom Jim talked warned him that the Indians would run off his stage horses, so he bought four hundred mules. When word of this got about, people began to call the San Antonio-San Diego Stageline the "Jackass Mail." Jim didn't know that Indians, although they scorned to ride muleback, considered mule meat delicious eating. The stageline stood to lose as much stock as if horses had been used.

The stagecoaches were canvas-covered wagons. Each trip along the rough track took

thirty days, and the fare each way was one
hundred fifty dollars. It was customary for
western stagelines to have two kinds of relay
stations: swing stations, where the stagecoach
stopped only long enough to have horses
changed, and home stations, where meals were
served to passengers. All the stations on the
Birch stageline were crude and widely scat-
tered. Most nights the stagedriver and passengers camped near a spring or water hole
while the six mules grazed. The passengers
chopped wood, carried water, and cooked their
meals over an open fire. They took turns
standing guard at night, for fear of an attack

by hostile Indians, and they rolled out of their blankets at dawn and helped harness the mules. It took a hardy person to travel by the Jackass Mail!

Besides taking his own blankets and food, a Jackass Mail passenger went heavily armed with a rifle and a Colt revolver. Small bands of Indians raided the line frequently. Desert travel was hard on the stage wagons and the drivers seldom stopped to make repairs. The sound of wagon wheels screaming for grease carried far on the clear air, and the Indians always knew when a stage wagon was coming.

Stagecoaching and mail delivery by Jackass Mail were exciting but chancy. This was because Jim Birch hadn't been given enough time to organize his stageline properly before putting it on the road. In time he probably would have overcome all the obstacles, but the San Antonio-San Diego Stageline had scarcely started when Jim Birch died.

Jim Birch will be remembered as the great pioneer of cross-country stagecoaching. But when Jim died, John Butterfield, an even greater stageman, had already stepped into the scene to carry out the great adventure that Jim had begun.

## 5. John Butterfield and the Ox-Bow Route

The Jackass Mail continued to struggle along without Jim Birch, but it was undependable. The Government finally decided that some more reliable mail and passenger service must be established between the eastern states and the states and territories of the West.

From his office in New York, John Butterfield had eagerly followed the activity of the Jackass Mail. He also studied the progress of several small stagelines which were trying, without much success, to pioneer routes across the central plains. John had been waiting for the right time to get into the challenging business of western transportation. Now he was sure that the time had come. He founded a new company, which he called the Butterfield Overland Mail, and he put in a bid to carry mail to California. His fame as a stageman was so great that he easily obtained a contract, but he had to promise to follow the route chosen by the Post Office Department.

The Postmaster General was a Southerner, and he was determined that the Overland Mail must run from Missouri and Tennessee and, in part, along the Birch route to California. Although John had been hoping for a more central route, he accepted this one. Then, in order to be close to the starting point of his westbound stagecoaches, he moved his office to St. Louis, Missouri.

John's contract gave him just a year in which to get twice-weekly mails running to and from California. The contract stated that each trip of two thousand miles must be made in not more than twenty-five days. This meant that sixteen stagecoaches must be on the road at all times—eight traveling west, and eight traveling east. In order to keep to the time schedule, they would have to travel a steady

one hundred and twelve miles a day through the roughest kind of country. Over most of this route there were no inns or even farms, so way stations would have to be built.

It was the most gigantic task ever attempted in American transportation, but John Butterfield set his firm jaw and tore into it.

His partner, Marcus Kinyon, immediately set to work in San Francisco preparing the western end of the line. At the same time, Bill Buckley, a trusted employee, left the East with a train of supply wagons and a work

The 2,000 mile route of the Overland Mail stretched from 1) Tipton, Missouri to 2) San Francisco.

crew to select a route and to build way stations.

The Pacific Railroad Company had finished a track as far as Tipton, a town 160 miles west of St. Louis, so John Butterfield made Tipton the eastern starting point of the Butterfield Overland Mail. The western starting point would be San Francisco.

From Tipton the route would run through Missouri, a corner of Arkansas, Indian Territory (as Oklahoma was then called), Texas, and

New Mexico Territory to Southern California where it would then follow the road to San Francisco.

The Ox-Bow route crossed wide stretches of blazing hot desert where water holes were far apart. The hard-working Butterfield crews dug wells for some of the dry stations, but others would have to be supplied with water by tank wagons.

Oats and hay for the stock and food for the passengers would have to be transported great distances by wagon to the isolated stations.

Although the eastern end of the route passed through the territory of friendly Choctaw and Cherokee Indians, the stations across Texas and Arizona were always in danger of raids by Comanches and Apaches who rightfully resented the intrusion of Americans into their hunting grounds. The stations on this part of the route were built like small forts, and the men on the supply wagons were heavily armed. John Butterfield had instructed his men to stay on friendly terms with the Indians, but he also wanted them to be prepared to defend themselves.

Keeping an anxious eye on the calendar, John hired a number of crack reinsmen to drive the Butterfield Overland stagecoaches. Some of them had worked for him in New York; others he recruited from California stagelines. Two hundred and fifty Concord stagecoaches were ordered from Downing and Abbot. Half of these were shipped by clipper to San Francisco, and the rest were taken to Tipton by railroad. John also bought over a thousand splendid horses and hundreds of sturdy mules. And he did not neglect to order the grease pots that would swing between the back wheels of every stagecoach. Firm orders went out from headquarters that the axles and wheel hubs must be greased at every stop. No Butterfield stagecoach was to go screeching across the country!

The stageline would use standard Concord stagecoaches on the eastern and California ends of the route, but for the rough wild country in between, John designed some special stagecoaches. He called them "celerity wagons," and they were to become widely used in the West. Downing and Abbot made them with the same skilled craftsmanship that went into their other Concord coaches.

A celerity wagon had a canvas top and sides, and it was longer than a standard Concord

A newspaper artist who traveled by Overland Mail drew this picture of a short stop on the prairie.

coach. Leather curtains hung at the windows. The padded leather seats had backs that could be folded down to make a platform on which passengers could sleep. There were no overnight stops for Overland Mail passengers; only short stops for meals and to change horses.

To insure efficiency in operating the stageline, Mr. Butterfield divided the route into nine divisions and placed an experienced manager over each division. Under each manager were station agents responsible for running their stations capably.

Newspapers all over the United States were keeping their readers informed of the preparations for getting the Butterfield Overland Mail on the road. Some people thought that the stagecoaches would fail to keep up the terrific speed of 112 miles a day every day in the year. But others remembered the famous motto of John Butterfield's New York stagelines: "Nothing on God's earth must stop the United States Mail!"

Soon it would be seen whether on western runs the new stageline could live up to those brave words.

If the stagecoaches fell behind the time schedule demanded by the Postmaster General, the line would lose its mail contracts. And the cost of running that far-flung stageline was so great that the company would have to go out of business if the contracts were withdrawn.

## 6. Mr. Ormsby Travels by the Overland Mail

It was early in the morning of September 16, 1858. At the St. Louis railroad station, smoke was puffing up from the chunky stack of the Tipton train. On the platform, John Butterfield pulled out his big gold watch and checked the time. In a few moments the train would pull out, and he had to be on it with the first westbound mail!

His face brightened as a mail wagon came rattling down the street. The driver was the St. Louis postmaster. He pulled his horse up beside the platform and took two leather pouches from the wagon. They were labeled: San Francisco, California. Per Overland Mail.

The postmaster handed the pouches to Mr. Butterfield.

"All aboard!" shouted the train conductor.

John crossed the platform with long strides.

"Good luck!" the postmaster called after him.

With its bell clanging, the train chugged out of the station along the track leading west along the Missouri River.

John chose a seat opposite one occupied by a well-dressed young man. This man had watched through the train window while John took over the mail pouches. Now he leaned across the aisle. "Mr. Butterfield . . . ."

John nodded pleasantly.

"I am Waterman Ormsby of the New York *Herald.* I have a ticket to San Francisco on the first Overland Mail."

The two men shook hands. Mr. Ormsby explained that he planned to write letters to his editor and send them to New York by the eastbound stagecoaches he would meet on the road. The letters would be published in the *Herald* to keep people informed about the first trip of the Butterfield Overland Mail.

The train arrived at Tipton at 6:00 P.M. A broad smile brightened John Butterfield's face when he saw the Concord stagecoach drawn up behind six spirited, pawing horses. In gold over the door were the words "Overland Mail." On the door was a gold eagle and the words "U.S. Mail."

John Butterfield, Jr. was on the box of the stagecoach. The conductor was waiting on the platform. He took the mail pouches from Mr. Butterfield and stowed them away in the forward luggage boot.

There were five other passengers waiting to board the stagecoach. The conductor collected their tickets and got everyone seated. Then he swung onto the box and blew a musical blast on the stagehorn. John, Jr.'s whip snaked out with a sharp *crack!* The horses surged forward in a gallop, and the Butterfield Overland Mail whirled away on the first stage of its long journey. As they got under way, John Butterfield was hoping that the eastbound Overland Mail would make as fine a start from California.

John, Jr. kept his horses at a gallop all the seven miles to the first relay station. The speeding stagecoach swayed and rocked, and John, Sr. kept putting his head outside the window, shouting to his son to take it easy.

"It's all right, Father!" young John shouted back.

He was in perfect control of his fiery team, and he was determined to make a record for his end of the line.

At the eastern end of the route, farmhouses often served as relay stations. Eager to be off and away, Mr. Butterfield often stepped out of the stagecoach to help with the task of changing horses.

In Springfield, Missouri, mail and passengers were transferred to a celerity wagon which would be used until the Overland Mail reached California.

John, Jr. held the reins as the Overland Mail began its long journey westward from Tipton.

The next day the stagecoach whirled along the twisting roads of the Ozark Mountains. Some of the down grades were so steep that the men fastened drags made of chains and tree trunks to the rear wheels to help the brakes hold the stagecoach back. That night they crossed the dark Arkansas River on a flatboat. The next stop was at Fort Smith on the border of Indian Territory, as Oklahoma was then called. There they connected with a stagecoach from Memphis, Tennessee, which had brought more mail for California.

John Butterfield and all the passengers, except Waterman Ormsby, left the stagecoach at Fort Smith. All were weary after three days of ceaseless traveling, but everyone was proud because the trip to Fort Smith had been made in the fastest time ever traveled by a stagecoach.

Mr. Ormsby was alone in the stagecoach when it left Fort Smith just before dawn. On the box sat a new driver and a new conductor. The driver would change every time they reached a new division, but the conductor would go straight through to San Francisco. In a voice husky with emotion, John Butterfield bade the three men good-bye.

Handing Mr. Ormsby a large basket, he said, "I had them put you up some lunch at the hotel." Then he looked up at the men on the box. "Remember boys, nothing on God's earth must stop the United States Mail!"

"Don't worry, Boss." The driver's whip cracked, and the team started off at a thundering gallop.

Hours later, Waterman Ormsby opened his lunch basket. He found a generous supply of sliced ham, crackers, cheese, some delicious cakes, and "ale to wash it down." He handed some of the food up to the driver and conductor, then settled back to enjoy his lunch while they whirled along. That night he tried the sleeping arrangements for the first time. He folded down the tops of the seats, rolled himself in a blanket, and stretched out. He fell asleep to the sound of trotting hoofs, jingling harness chains, and whirring wheels. At dawn the celerity wagon bumped across a log bridge and woke him. He rolled up the window curtain and murmured with surprise as he watched the landscape speed past. He certainly hadn't expected to see such well-tended farms and comfortable log houses in Indian Territory.

All through Indian Territory the Butterfield Overland Mail used farmhouses for way stations. In his news letters, Mr. Ormsby noted the good service and delicious meals received from the friendly Indian employees of "Big Chief Butterfield."

Through the open windows he could see grassy plains where Indian cowboys and great herds of cattle marked the beginning of the West. As the stagecoach sped onward, he thought about the vast lonely wilderness ahead and wondered anxiously if the Butterfield Mail could indeed keep up to the rugged time schedule demanded by the Postmaster General.

## 7. On to California

The muddy Red River formed the boundary line between Indian Territory and Texas. The stagecoach crossed the river on a raft pushed by two Indians wielding poles. Then it bore west across the Texas plains.

Many of the way stations along this lonely stretch had yet to be built. The widely spaced home stations were mostly primitive log cabins. Sometimes a meal consisted only of black coffee, served in tin cups, and shortcake, a kind of bread baked over the fireplace coals, sometimes on the blade of a hoe. It was a red-letter day when the travelers had a meal of bacon or beefsteak. At one station, chickens wandered in and out on the dirt floor. The agent urged Mr. Ormsby and his companions to "Hurry up and eat before the hens get the food!"

On this part of the route, mules were used for the stagecoach teams, and at one relay station they were so wild that they had to be lassoed in the corral and dragged to the stagecoach. One broke away and went bucking across the plain, madly pursued by the yelling station agent with his twirling lasso. Finally, with all the men straining and pulling and the mules rearing, kicking, and braying, the struggling animals were harnessed to the celerity wagon. Nervously, Mr. Ormsby climbed inside.

"Hija-ha, ha! Git-up there, ol' mule!" yelled the driver.

The mules started at a fast trot that soon became a headlong run. When the stagedriver tried to pull them in, they fought the reins and began to plunge, rear, and buck, jerking the stagecoach this way and that. The stagecoach rocked alarmingly and then turned over with a crash, and one of the mules kicked a hole in the top. Just before the crash,

Mr. Ormsby made a flying leap out the window. The driver and conductor tumbled from their seats and sprawled upon the prairie grass.

Mr. Ormsby grimly helped get the stagecoach upright.

"If I had any property to leave, I'd certainly make a hasty will," he wrote gloomily to his editor, as they started off again.

But the mules seemed to have worked off their wildness. They settled down to a steady trot as the moon rose to light the lonely trail.

When the stagecoach reached the desert country of west Texas, the sand and scarcity of water slowed the speed of the mule teams. Until now the Overland Mail had stayed ahead of its schedule, but now everyone began to worry about losing time. The blazing heat of the sun was almost unbearable. The wheels hissed in the sand that blew across the sun-baked road, and the tired mules pulled heavily. Stops were made for the animals and men to drink canteen water. The axles and wheel hubs were greased frequently.

The lonely road was marked by the skeletons of men and of horses, mules, and oxen who had died of heat and thirst. These gruesome remains were a warning to the travelers that they, too, could come to such an end if their water gave out or the stagecoach broke down. Their hearts thrilled with thankfulness when at last they came to the relay station on the bank of the Pecos River. Waterman Ormsby went without dinner that day in order to take a bath in the swift, sparkling river. He soaked while the team was changed, then he flung on his clothes, grabbed a chunk of cornbread, and sprinted to the coach.

One hundred miles east of El Paso, Texas, on September 28, 1858, the Butterfield Overland Mail from the East met the first eastbound Mail from San Francisco. The conductors fired a salute from their guns, and Mr. Ormsby and the eastbound passengers let out a hearty cheer. Mr. Ormsby handed over to the conductor of the other stagecoach his letters to his editor; then the two celerity wagons rolled past each other, going east and west.

The road now led through Apache country. The Indians did not attack the stagecoach because Cochise, one of the two chiefs of the Apache Nation, had promised to let the "swift-wagons" of "Chief Butterfield" pass unharmed. Mangas Colorados, the other chief, was not so friendly, but he too had agreed not to attack.

Passengers felt lucky when they were able to stop at a home station for a hot meal served at a table.

But Mangas Colorados knew that swift-wagons meant way stations stocked with mules and food. He and a party of his warriors had already called at one of the Butterfield Stations. The chief demanded ten bags of corn, and the alarmed agent had promptly handed the corn over. The Indians rode away, but they did not promise not to return!

Day and night the stagecoach rolled westward. Beyond the Rio Grande the bold peaks of the Guadalupe Mountains pierced the sky. At dusk, in gloomy Guadalupe Canyon, the westbound stagecoach met the second Overland

Mail from San Francisco. It did everyone good to know that the Ox-Bow route was operating smoothly from both ends.

"We travel day and night," wrote Mr. Ormsby, "only stopping to eat and change teams."

They made the perilous crossing of the Colorado River on a flatboat. The boat was kept on course through the swift, wild water by pulleys running on a rope that stretched across the river. The pitching boat, the frightened mules, and the rocking and sliding of the stagecoach seemed like a nightmare.

Gaunt, weary, and dirty from their rugged journey, Waterman Ormsby and his companions finally arrived in California. At a way station in a picturesque old Spanish mission, they exchanged their battered celerity wagon and mules for a shining scarlet Concord stagecoach and six spendid horses. Then, with Waterman Ormsby still the lone westbound passenger, they started off at a gallop.

On Sunday, October 10, Mr. Ormsby wrote in his news letter: "It was just after sunrise that the city of San Francisco hove in sight over the hills . . . ."

Soon the hoofs of the horses were pounding on city pavements. They clattered into San Francisco Plaza and stopped in front of the post office. The conductor blew a resounding blast on his stagehorn, then, with the mail pouches in his hands, he strode up to the door of the post office and pounded on it impatiently.

"Hi there!" he shouted. "Open up! The Overland Mail from the East has arrived!"

With a happy grin, Waterman Ormsby noted that they had made the trip in 23 days and 23½ hours.

The Butterfield Overland Mail need worry no longer about losing its mail contracts!

## 8. Ben Holladay
### and the Central Overland Stage Line

After that successful first run, the Butterfield Overland Mail continued to give dependable service for two and a half years. Every stagecoach was crowded with passengers and mail. But then, in 1860, John Butterfield retired. The men who succeeded him as managers of the line were less experienced than he in stagecoaching. This was the beginning of the bad luck that now beset the Ox-Bow route.

An ignorant army lieutenant insulted the great Apache chief Cochise, making Cochise a bitter enemy of the Americans. Stagecoach travel was stopped in Arizona as the chief savagely swept the white intruders from his land. Back east, the Civil War had begun.

Western posts were stripped of soldiers to swell the Union Army; there were few troops left to protect travelers in the West.

Beset by both Confederate soldiers and hostile Indians, the division managers of the Butterfield Overland Mail decided to move the line north into Utah. Some of the stations had been destroyed by Indians. Without waiting for orders from faraway headquarters, the stagemen themselves set fire to the stations that were left, before setting out on their perilous journey. As the caravan of stagemen, stagecoaches, horses, and mules traveled north, smoke from the burning Butterfield stations curled up into the sky behind them, marking the end of the Ox-Bow Route, a gallant adventure in stagecoaching.

In Utah the Butterfield Overland Mail Company was taken over by Wells, Fargo. This great banking and express company of California was extending its stagelines to Nevada and Utah. The new Butterfield headquarters were in Salt Lake City, and the stageline ran through the mountains of Nevada to connect with Wells, Fargo stagelines in California. Now a new stageline was needed to connect the East with this western line.

Next stop Virginia City! The last leg of the journey for eager miners was by Wells, Fargo stagecoach.

Ranches, towns, and mining camps had sprung up in the wake of the western pioneers. The problem of passenger and mail transportation was greater than ever.

A number of small stagecoach lines had been struggling to operate east of Salt Lake City but they had not prospered, mainly because they did not have mail contracts. Now the most important of these stagelines was bought by a big, bearded man whose shrewd eyes had the glint of steel.

Ben Holladay was as hard and tough as the untamed country in which he worked. Like

John Butterfield, he was a genius at organization, but unlike John, he had no real love for stagecoaching. To him a stageline was simply a means of making money. Ben had friends in the government, and he lost no time in securing mail contracts for his new stageline. It was called the Overland Stage Line.

Horses were important to him only because his stagecoaches could not run without them. On the Overland, many a fine horse was ruined by being overworked. Passengers were even less important to Ben than horses. He knew that people had to ride in his stagecoaches if they wanted to get anywhere east of Salt Lake, and he wasted no time in worrying about their comfort. Passengers complained bitterly of being jolted and bruised in overloaded old stagecoaches. One man wrote that he had crossed the plains in a coach that had only two floor boards left in it.

"Pack 'em in! Pack 'em in like sardines!" was Ben's watchword.

Passengers complained also about the poor and scanty food at Overland way stations. On his inspection trips, Ben always traveled with his own provisions and a chef, so he wouldn't have to eat the food served to his passengers.

Mark Twain wrote a book called *Roughing It* in which he told about some of his experiences traveling in an Overland stagecoach!

"We began to get into country threaded with streams with steep high banks. Every time we flew down one bank and scrambled up the other, our party got mixed up somewhat. First we would all be down in a pile at the forward end of the stage . . . and in a second we would shoot to the other end and stand on our heads."

But stagecoach travel had a delightful side for Mark Twain also.

"The coach swayed and swung . . . the breeze flapping the curtains in a most exhilarating way. The pattering of the horses' hoofs, the cracking of the driver's whip, and his 'Hi-yi, g'lang' were music . . . . Even to this day it thrills me to think of . . . those fine Overland mornings."

In the 1860's the Overland Stage Line was

hit hard by white desperadoes who held up stagecoaches and stole horses, and by Indians who were angry because more and more white settlers kept pouring west to settle on their lands and to kill off the buffalo. The Sioux and other tribes attacked way stations, burned tons of hay, and ran off hundreds of Ben Holladay's stage horses.

During these times of peril and bloodshed, stagecoach drivers showed unflinching courage and devotion to duty. One stagecoach, traveling east from Nevada, was attacked by a band of Indians as it arrived at a way station.

The Indians had already captured the station and killed the agent and the cook. Then they hid behind the wall of the corral and waited for the stagecoach to come along.

Hank Harper, one of the finest reinsmen in the West, was driving the stagecoach. On the box beside him sat John Liverton, a passenger. Judge Mott, a congressman, was asleep inside, and sitting across from him were the two little Liverton boys.

As the stagecoach dashed up to the station, Hank was surprised that the agent was not waiting with the relay team. Then his keen eyes noted that there were Indian ponies in the

corral with the company horses. His whip cracked out over his team.

"Get along there!" he roared.

The team broke into a gallop, and the stage-coach whirled past the station in a cloud of dust. The Indians flung themselves on their ponies and stormed in pursuit. War cries split the air and arrows and bullets sped toward the stagecoach. A bullet struck John Liverton. His body fell across the footboard. Several bullets hit Hank Harper; he pitched forward and slid into the boot. But he kept a tight grip on the reins.

Driven wild by the gunfire and yelling, the horses plunged off the road and tore across the plain. The stagecoach rocked and bumped crazily behind them. The commotion awakened Judge Mott. He peered out of the window, then hastily pushed the boys to the floor.

Although he was weak from pain and loss of blood, Hank managed a croaking shout. "Get up here, Judge! I can't hold out much longer!"

The Judge squeezed himself through the stagecoach window. He was a tall man and he managed to reach up and grasp the iron railing running around the top of the Concord. Several arrows struck near him, and bullets zinged past his ears as he pulled himself up and, on his hands and knees, crawled along the roof of the madly rocking stagecoach. At last he clambered down to the box and took the reins from Hank's tired hands.

"I've never driven a team before," he confessed worriedly.

"Now's the time for you to learn!" Hank rasped.

Somehow Hank found the strength to cling to the edge of the boot and talk to his horses, soothing and directing them and helping the

Judge get them back on the road. The next station, a strongly fortified place, was eight miles away.

"If we can get there, we'll be safe," Hank whispered.

The team responded nobly to the voice of their driver and the strong hands of the Judge. They fairly flew along, leaving the Indian ponies far behind. When the station came in sight, Hank sighed, and his hands let go their desperate grip on the boot. The Judge had to use all his strength to pull the frothing team to a halt.

The people at the station came rushing out to help. They found that Mr. Liverton was still alive, although badly wounded. The boys were unhurt. But Hank Harper was dead.

He had died true to the heroic tradition of great stagedrivers. He had brought his passengers safely to the next station.

## 9. Sunset Time for Stagecoaching

Ever since the first rails had been laid in the East, Americans had been hoping for a transcontinental railroad that would bind their country together. Construction of this railroad had lagged during the Civil War, but as soon as the war was over, it was speeded up. By 1866, tracks had been laid as far west as Omaha, Nebraska.

Shrewd, ruthless Ben Holladay had made millions in stagecoaching because of his mail contracts and his pinchpenny treatment of passengers. Now the stagecoach king realized that stagecoaching could not compete with the

railroad much longer. In 1860 he sold the Overland Stage Line to Wells, Fargo.

In California and on their mountain runs to Salt Lake City, Wells, Fargo had made a magnificent success of stagecoaching. Now, as soon as they acquired the rundown Holladay Line, they overhauled it and brought it up to the standard of their other lines. Fares were reduced. New horses replaced the overworked Holladay teams. Thirty new Concord stage-coaches were ordered from Downing and Abbot.

As late as 1868 Wells, Fargo ordered this shipment
of thirty Concord stagecoaches from Abbot, Downing.

Wells, Fargo stagelines now ran from
California to Missouri, but people who traveled
in them saw the tracks of the Union Pacific
Railroad stretch farther west and east each
day. Everyone knew that when the tracks met
in Utah it would mean the end of transcontinental stagecoaching.

The usefulness of stagecoaches did not end
suddenly. For years after the last spike in the
railroad was driven in 1869, stagecoaches

continued to give service on branch lines connecting with the railroad.

During those years there was plenty of adventure in the changing West. Indian nations were still unconquered and free-roaming. Grizzly bears took naps in the middle of the stagecoach road. Vast herds of buffalo poured across the roads and sometimes held up stagecoaches and railroads for hours. Holdup men waited for stagecoaches to come along mountain roads with treasure chests from the mines. And until the wheels of the last stagecoach ceased to turn, the jaunty courageous stagedrivers were the heroes of every boy who saw them or read about them.

# Glossary

**bid:** an offer to do a job for a stated price

**boot:** deep luggage carrier of a stagecoach

**box:** the stagedriver's seat

**celerity wagon:** a stagecoach used in rough country

**conductor:** the person who rode with the driver of a stagecoach and collected fares, took care of passengers, and had charge of the mail

**diggings:** place where gold or other metal ore was mined

**drag:** object attached to the back of a stagecoach to slow it when going downhill

**home station:** station at which meals were served to passengers

**johnnycake:** a kind of corn bread

**joiner:** a carpenter who finishes inside woodwork such as doors, molding, etc.

**mustang:** a wild, small horse found in the Southwest

**overland:** across land rather than by water

**postrider:** a mail carrier who traveled by horseback between specific places

**reinsman:** a stagedriver

**relay:** a team of horses kept in readiness at a way station to relieve the team of an approaching stagecoach

**run:** the distance between stations on a stagecoach journey

**stagehorn:** a horn blown by the conductor as the stage neared the station

**stageline:** a stagecoach company

**station:** the place at which a stagecoach stopped—see **swing station** and **home station**

**swing station:** a station where only horses were changed

**transcontinental:** across the United States

**turnpike:** a main road on which travelers paid a toll or fee

**way station:** same as **station**

**waybills:** advertisements for stagelines posted in towns and villages

**wheelwright:** a person who makes or fixes wheels

# Index